P9-CLU-594

On Seeing Nature

On Seeing Nature

STEVEN J. MEYERS

Fulcrum, Inc. • 1987

Copyright © 1987
Fulcrum, Incorporated

Book and Cover Design By
Frederick R. Rinehart

LIBRARY OF CONGRESS
CATALOGING-IN-PUBLICATION DATA
Meyers, Steven J.
On Seeing Nature
1. Nature   2. Nature – Philosophy
I. Title
QB81.M584   1987   508'01'3   86-25784
ISBN 1-55591-008-4

FULCRUM, INC.
GOLDEN, COLORADO

For Daniel

CONTENTS

Acknowledgements

No one lives or works in a vacuum. In a very real sense all of our products are the shared creations of humankind, and, as I hope will be apparent to readers of this book, all of nature. Still, there are certain people without whose very specific and direct help some projects would never reach completion. These I would like to thank directly.

First I would like to thank my family, specifically my father, I. Edward Meyers, who taught me to love and respect the natural world; my mother, Rose Meyers, whose unfailing support and affection have carried me through many projects, including the present book; and my brother, Dr. Harry P. Meyers, whose kindness, generosity and perceptive mind have served to represent all that people might become, all that people should strive to be.

I would like to thank Dr. Michael Zimmerman of Tulane University for his friendship, his thoughtful comments on preliminary drafts of the manuscript of this book, and the many conversations which directly influenced my thoughts on the seeing of nature. I would also like to thank Dolores LaChapelle, author and friend, whose ideas and profound wisdom have significantly altered my perceptions and experiences of nature.

Special gratitude is owed to Karen Boucher, my companion and love, without whose company life and the seeing of nature would lose their special glow. My debt to her transcends language, or at any rate my ability to use language. In no one else have I seen such affection for, or natural affinity with, living things, such ability to make all manner of life blossom – from the children she so lovingly teaches, to the plants she so gently tends in her many gardens. I and this book have bloomed under her care and affection as well.

Finally, I would like to thank my son Daniel. All parents see their children as special, extraordinary. I suppose it is good that we do. Can I be forgiven for thinking that my child is *really* special? Being with him, watching him grow, spending time with him in the woods, on foot, on skis, afloat in a canoe, I have come to understand nature and wonder in ways which might forever have escaped me had it not been for the incredible freshness of his childlike vision. More than anyone else he has left his imprint on this book. It is to him and his vision that the book is dedicated.

For any odd quirks, eccentric notions, or outright errors I take full responsibility; I admit to being quirky, eccentric and making an occasional mistake (well, maybe more than an occasional mistake). But I am willing to learn. And learning is what this book is all about.

ON SEEING NATURE

I. *Introduction*

WHEN MY SON was very young, too young to sustain an interest in fishing, we would go to the woods to a favorite place to spend time alone, together. Each of us would do what we pleased within sight of the other, but each of us was very much lost in his own perception of the place which we shared. On many of these trips I would fish for brook trout in the clear clean waters of Lime Creek, while Daniel would play in the sun-dappled forest which lined its banks. My attention would wander, but for the most part it would be trained on the rhythms of the stream: its structure, its water, its fish and insects. Likewise, Daniel's attention would wander, but the primary recipient of his attention would be the world of the forest floor: its plants and animals, humus and stones.

Every now and then we would share a ritual which would unite our two worlds of perception. When I would hook a fish, Daniel would come over to watch as I gently played it and then led it toward shore and calm shallow water. There we would join in the releasing of the fish. Daniel would place his hands under the fish to support it, while I would carefully twist the barbless hook of the fly from its mouth. Slowly I would step back to watch. Daniel would hold the fish as it gathered strength. He would wonder at the beauty of its brilliant spots and gently waving fins. His eyes would grow large in his seeing of the moment. Finally the fish would swim away, and we would look at each other. I would know that Daniel had seen the awesome beauty of life, had held it, throbbing, in his hands, and that I had seen him much the same as he had seen the trout. Then we would quietly go back to being alone, together, in this favorite part of the woods.

A few years later, when impatience and the need to be constantly running, jumping and tossing stones had partially left him, when the desire to become a competent fisherman in his own right had taken hold of him, we spent an afternoon fishing together at a small mountain lake. Not long after our arrival we began to cast small spinners into the shallow waters surrounding the rocky point on which we stood. In a matter of minutes Daniel hooked his first fish, a spirited rainbow trout who clearly wanted nothing to do with captivity. Bravely he fought the pull of the line and the bite of the hook, but Daniel's persistence overcame him. As we held the fish in shallow water, I asked Daniel if he would like to release the fish. Full of pride, he answered no. This was his fish, and he intended to take it home to show everyone. Carefully we released the hook from the trout's mouth, and placed him on a stringer.

We continued to fish, but I noticed that Daniel's concentration had been broken. More and more he wandered over to the water we had chosen as a holding place for Daniel's trout. The fish moved slowly, opening and closing his mouth against the uncomfortable stringer, forcing water through his gills so that he would not suffocate. It was clear that the fish had lost none of his beauty for having been taken, and none of his desire to live.

I could see a great sadness come over Daniel. When I asked him what was wrong his eyes filled with tears, and he asked if it would be all right to release the fish. I said that I thought that would be a good thing to do. We removed the stringer, held the fish, and watched as he gathered strength and realized that he was free. Finally we cheered as he swam into deep water, perhaps more aware

ON SEEING NATURE

of fishermen than he had been before, and hopefully less likely to be caught again.

Daniel's tears had grown into torrents by now, and his quiet voice had broken down into sobs. Between sobs he asked if we had hurt the fish, if it was silly of him to cry. He wanted to know if he could ever be a fisherman if he didn't want to kill fish. I don't remember what I said to him in answer to his questions, but I do remember holding him and telling him how proud I was of what he had done.

Seeing begins with respect. There are as many ways to learn respect, I suppose, as there are ways to see, but it is clear that no one can truly see something he has not respected. Respect for the natural world, however, is a tricky thing. With respect comes an overwhelming desire for understanding, and, with the beginnings of understanding, a sometimes erroneous belief that we have a legitimate empathy. We understand, at first, by projecting our own needs and desires, our own perceptions, into the world which confronts us. Yet, if we are to see on the basis of what is, and not what we wish there to be, our understanding must transcend our own limited experience. Is this possible?

The problem of seeing nature, of truly perceiving what is there, is not unlike the significantly less complex problem of accurately seeing another human being. When we are confronted with the reality of understanding another person, the dimensions of the problem seem immense. Even with those we love, those we know best, there are private areas of meaning and perception which cannot be articulated, and never fully understood. When we allow the question of understanding to grow and include not just loved ones and friends, but those we hardly know at all, the scope of our ignorance, the questions regarding the accuracy of our seeing, grow immeasurably. Then there is the chasm which exists between ourselves and those who belong to cultures which are radically different in values and lifestyle from our own. Do we ever really see them? Would we dare to suppose that empathy between us is possible? How dare we suppose that we might be able to truly see or understand organisms which are not even of our own species? What of inanimate reality? What arrogance exists in the hope to see nature?

Seeing starts with respect. Respect doesn't come from the depth of our understanding of another individual, or organism, or ecosystem, or nature as a whole. In every instance the scope of our ignorance vastly overshadows that of our knowledge. Respect comes from a belief that the great abyss of our ignorance, a void articulated by the sketchy understanding we possess, contains meaning worthy of our attention and effort, no matter how difficult the task appears. No matter how brilliant a naturalist one might be, no matter how perceptive and observant one might become, one's knowledge must never overcome one's awe. If it should, the contents of that knowledge become suspect. As long as there is awe, there is seeing.

I have no doubt that Daniel's sense of wonder grew in his first encounter with a living brook trout, in his seeing of its spots and the waving of its fins, in his feeling of the movement of life in his hands. I am just as certain that each subsequent encounter enriched his wonder. His sadness for the captured trout that pride would have killed, and which empathy released, was full of human ignorance and projection, the same ignorance and projection that we adults indulge. It was also full of respect. A respect which belied his youth, and demonstrated true seeing.

Seeing nature is a process, partly, of replacing our arrogance with humility. When we respect the reality which fills the abyss of our ignorance, we begin to see.

If respect is basic, how important is wonder? Seeing begins with respect, but wonder is the fuel which sustains vision. To most of us the reality of wonder, its presence in our everyday lives, has become diminished in the process of growing up. The extraordinary has become ordinary, the unfamiliar, familiar, the incredible, credible. We expect that the sun will rise each morning, that spring will follow winter, that the world which grows dark when we close our eyes will reappear when we open them. It is a rare adult who thinks about these things. We forget that it has not always been so.

An infant's sense of wonder is boundless, a child's scarcely less. As unusual as the adult who would sit watching clouds form and dissolve is the child who wouldn't. It is this wonder which emerges as a child confronts the outside world that causes children to explore and learn. And it is familiarity which gradually dims the child's wonder as he becomes an adult. We become people who filter everything through previous experience, seeing less and learning little. It is not the ability to see which has fled; all the ingredients remain. What has leaked out is the fuel that powers the visual apparatus – the sense of wonder.

This book is about seeing nature, and a few of the ingredients necessary for that task have been mentioned. First, I said that it was necessary to respect nature, not on the basis of presumed knowledge, but rather, with an attitude of humility which recognizes our great ignorance. Next, I said that a proper response to the abyss of our ignorance, and the respect we feel for the reality we sense, would be an attitude of awe. What now exists to help us overcome our ignorance and fear in the face of the unknown? The answer is simple: childlike wonder. Fortunately, nature has an enormous capacity to inspire wonder. If we respond to this inspiration we will look, and we will see.

As Daniel held that trout in his hands, as his eyes grew wide with wonder, I too was filled with wonder, and my eyes grew wide as well. Daniel throbbed no less, his spots were no less beautiful; children are no less wonderful than trout, and no less a part of nature.

The distance which grows between so many adults and the natural world, a world in which we fit so comfortably as children, grows slowly and imperceptibly. Gradually this distance robs us of our respect, our awe, and our wonder. It diminishes much more than our capacity to see. It steals our joy. The desire to see nature is more than the desire to see phenomena. It is the desire to regain ourselves, to perceive the context which nourishes and sustains us, which provides meaning for us and, most significantly, brings pleasure to our lives.

II. Learning to See

LEARNING TO SEE is a complex process, and in many ways it mirrors other kinds of human development. This question of how we learn to see has been the focal point of many a hot debate in the fields of human development, learning theory, perceptual psychology and physiology. The details of the discussion are best left to experts, but what we can do away from the specialized worlds of the developmental psychologist, the perceptual researcher, the learning theorist, the neuro-physiologist, the geneticist, the anatomist and the molecular biologist is to examine some simple observations about seeing. From our experiences with others, from introspection about our own growth, observing creatures, we can make inferences regarding the process of seeing, and learning to see, which are valid and useful. In some ways, the broad perspective of the generalist is more illuminating than the focussed examination of the specialist.

There are many questions about the status of the visual apparatus at birth. Some of these questions involve the long-standing dispute between nature and nurture, between genetic determinism and learning. The fact that these questions have not been resolved with either nature or nurture becoming the single dominant factor corroborates the current feeling in biological study that this conflict has always been something of a red herring. Neither position can be held in the extreme without serious contradictions emerging. There is no question that significant genetic factors exist, and it is equally certain that learning modifies seeing. Recent study indicates that learning is strongly influenced by the structure of our bodies, and it is believed that this structure is the result of adaptations which have been genetically transmitted over time. Because of the genetic influence on the physical structure of the visual apparatus, our visual history begins not with our individual births but with the dawn of time.

This is a book about seeing, and learning to see in new ways. Its hope for success rests on the assumption that our connection with our evolutionary past, a past perhaps more significantly influential than we realize, has left us with perceptual ability that a life lived in isolation from the full breadth of nature cannot actualize. We would see so much more if only we would explore terrain which was common to our ancestors but which has become distant for most of us.

It is obvious that we are born with an apparatus which enables us to see, and we know from reflecting on past experience that the clarity of our vision grows with learning. We notice varying degrees of perceptual acuity in our own experience, and we infer that the process of change in perceptual ability occurs in others also as we watch them move through time, as we watch them grow. In watching children, friends, ourselves, we find abundant evidence of the growth of vision, of the effects of learning on our ability to see. We make a mistake, however, if we believe that the process becomes complete with maturation. As long as we seek growth, we continue to develop our capacity to see.

It is true that we are all born with certain limits to vision. Sometimes these limits are severe. The great tragedy of blindness however – or even of lesser physical disabilities like nearsightedness or astigmatism – are not the only limiting influences. Our attitudes, the things we are exposed to in the development of our visual capabilities, the values of those who influence our growth, the shared vision of the cultures which form our individual contexts, all of these affect the depth and breadth of our vision. To have our experience of nature severely limited, to have the value of vision and the seeing of nature reduced by context, is no less a tragedy than having been born blind. For some of us, blindness has become a way of life, even though the visual apparatus is intact. How much sadder all of this is, when we consider how easy it would be to reverse the process if somehow our value based blindness were made known.

In speaking about the seeing of nature, a great deal has been said, indirectly, about nature. If we are going to explore the seeing of nature, we need to discuss nature as well as seeing, therefore a definition of nature is in order.

A historian whom I greatly admire, Martin Duberman, once said that historians are not able to choose between having their values affect their work and writing value-free, objective history; instead, they must choose between showing their values directly or pretending that they do not exist at all. For Duberman, in history, in life, there was no such thing as objectivity. There was, however, a difference between honesty and deceit. In defining nature, I might take the seemingly objective approach of defining nature as it has been defined historically, or I might retreat to

the safety of the dictionary. I might quote others and avoid questions of value. But this would be less than honest. My definition of nature is as much a reflection of my values as a discussion of my views on ethics might be. Discussions and definitions tend to lapse into the third person, but I want to say at the outset that there is a being, in the first person, lurking behind my every word. What I would hope is that lurking behind the person there is also a world inhabited by much more than humankind, which has had a hand in the shaping of these definitions and discussions.

Nature, for me, is quite simply all that exists. This definition is rather plain, and possibly a bit confusing. Its sense lies, perhaps, in what it is not.

This is not a definition which allows one to distinguish between what is natural and what is not. For some nature is contrasted with the unnatural: plastic, internal-combustion engines, rocket ships, smog. If we look at typical examples of the unnatural, however, we find that what we really have is a separation into manmade and not manmade. To define nature in this way is to separate human products from the rest of nature. Is a tool made by a chimp natural in a way that one made by a man is not? Is a bird's nest natural while a person's home is not? To divide natural and unnatural in this way separates man from nature. It makes him somehow different, and in the worst case, makes him believe that by virtue of his separateness he is somehow better and therefore justified in doing as he pleases without regard for the consequences to the rest of what exists.

This is not a definition which associates the natural with the beautiful. For some, nature is pastoral, pleasant. It is broad vistas, blue skies, sweet air, clear water, virgin timber in lush forests, pristine snow on rolling fields, high peaks, the roar of the sea. It is not birds dying from human waste and toxins, children starving on the streets of Latin American cities, illness and death. Here the natural and the unnatural seem to be divided on the basis of the attractive and the unattractive, or on the basis of our notions of good and evil. Defining nature in this way we appear to be imposing a limited set of values upon nature. Once again we have separated man from nature; this time not in terms of fabrication, but in terms of ethical and aesthetic constructs. Is the death of a ground squirrel in the talons of a hawk

ON SEEING NATURE

evil? Is the vine which chokes a magnificent tree ugly? Certainly not in the eyes of the hawk, or the vine.

Nature includes all things that exist, all of the processes which connect them, all of the history which brought what is to its current state of existence, and the future which lies beyond. For man to exclude himself, or his products, or to impose his notions of the evil or the ugly from an external viewpoint, exempts him from responsibility as an agent acting within nature. If we value beauty, trees, pristine snow on rolling fields, if we hold and value constructs which include a notion of good and of evil, we would do well to realize that we are natural, and that our products are natural, that the trees we plant, and the poisons we create, all become part of the natural reality we inhabit and constitute.

In so defining nature, I have tried to avoid romanticizing the natural world, and although I am profoundly aware of my humanity, I have tried to avoid seeing nature through exclusively human needs and desires. If we become a part of nature, or more accurately, perceive ourselves to be the part of nature which we most certainly are, then the clarity of our seeing is greatly improved.

One notion which seems to broaden vision and aid in our seeing of nature (as well as helping us to define nature more accurately) is that of time. Our perception of the significance of man and his products changes when our notion of time transcends human experience and becomes framed in a broader history. Man has been around for a very short time.

If we travel in our minds back through human history, following a time line that examines our political and scientific achievements, we marvel at the generations which have passed, the lives lived, the happiness and sadness, the pleasure and pain which mankind has experienced. If we continue to go back, we reach a time when political and scientific accomplishments cease to have meaning. We reach a point where all we have are vague imaginings about early man and primitive life. The time spanned to get to this point is immense, yet it is nothing, really, on the calendar of human evolution. How many thousands of years ago did politics and science as we know them come to be? How many tens of thousands of years did man live without them? How many hundreds of thousands of years did he hunt and gather, and relocate with climatic change? How many millions of years did it take for him to slowly change from quadrapedal to bipedal, arboreal to terrestrial, from prototype primate to specified man? How many hundreds of millions of years ago did he breathe air for the first time? How many hundreds of millions of years were there between single cellular life and multicellular specialization, the development of organs, of complex species, of communities of species? With this unfathomable depth of time lying before us, can we even begin to think of these hundreds of millions of years as merely a thin dusting of time on top of the geological processes which came before life? How do we begin to think about the time of the cosmic processes which came before earthly geology? Are we capable of understanding the immensity of time which constitutes nature? Do we begin to realize how small a part of all of this man really is?

It may have come as a surprise to some that a book on seeing nature, written by an author who readily admits to having been deeply moved by the presence of a forest, the beauty and mystery of the sea, the emergence into view of a range of mountains when the summit of a high peak has been reached, would argue that smog and plastic and rocket ships are natural. They are, but the time has come to put them in perspective. We have made them, we are responsible for the consequences of their existence. Before we evaluate those consequences, however, I think we need to think about their place in time. We need to see them, and all of nature, with the wide eyes of a child who has contemplated the past, of an adult who knows the extraordinary thinness of the veneer that this layer we call human habitation represents upon the massive reality we call nature. To define nature we need a sense of perspective and a sense of time. We need these to see as well.

I have defined nature as all that exists, yet when I write about nature in this book, discussions of cities and industry will be noticeably absent. Is this inconsistent? I think not. Given man's place in nature, and the breadth of the history which constitutes natural reality, there really doesn't seem to be a great need to spend much time discussing cities or factories when the hope is to see nature. While the natural world constantly changes, and little remains which does not show the hand of man, it is my belief that there is a great deal more to be learned from the parts of nature with which we are least familiar than from those we have created and know best. Our familiarity with cities and industrialization already exceeds our need. Our ignorance of the rest is appalling.

Individual temperament significantly affects seeing, and any discussion of learning to see nature must deal with this fact. Whatever the roots of temperament, it is clear that we seem to be attracted to certain places, and that the special attractions vary from individual to individual. A part of seeing clearly is finding one's niche. From this niche one's vision expands readily, but I doubt many see well who have not found a place where they feel particularly at home. Are we born with residual longings for specialized habitats? Is this longing the result of the genetic transmission of selected traits? Or, is this degree of comfort with a place a learned response? I don't know, but once again, from my own experience and from my observations of others, it would appear that the fact of individuals finding some places more attractive than others is an undeniable occurrence.

Successful naturalists have often been those whose concerns and observations were dictated by, and in tune with their temperaments. Some biologists are attracted in an almost magical way to the tropical rain forest, where a myriad of species is studied in a special environment. Others seem attracted to more limited, almost abstracted environments like arctic tundra. Some are attracted to specific life forms, birds for example, wherever they may be found. Still others find a home somewhere, a place where they are comfortable, and in this home they look at everything that happens. They see the weather, and begin to sense its changes. They see its plant life and recognize the groups in which they occur and the specialized microclimates which allow them to exist. They see the animal communities which thrive within or move through several of these plant systems. Their home begins to appear as an organism, and not as an assemblage of individuals. For some, this interrelatedness and the clarity of vision which it produces is global, but I believe they are the exception. For the rest of us, there are a few special places within which we feel at home. In them we find sufficient complexity to inspire our interest, and a magical comfort from which to work. Surely it is possible to expand one's vision, to see the broad context, the greater reality, but I can think of no better place to start than the place where one feels at home.

It would be silly for one who loves the seacoast but feels uncomfortable in the desert to first examine and explore the natural world in the desert. Those who love the lushness of the forest, and find that the isolation of tundra and altitude cause sadness or fear would learn little, initially, in the exploration of high mountains. First, I think, we must explore our homes, our places of special attraction. After this, we may tap the special lessons of the unfamiliar, and even the uncomfortable.

I have heard it argued that great scientists have a system of thought which would successfully guide the examination of any phenomenon, any complex collection of phenomena. For the most part, I reject this notion. My reading of human inquiry, of the history of science and of nature study in particular, is that those who have seen clearly and in novel ways are those who worked hard in a place which they found particularly comfortable, in a place which suited them temperamentally. For some extraordinary scientists this home was unusually large. For Darwin the entire world seemed to be home. Einstein seemed strangely comfortable with thoughts about the mind of God. Linus Pauling with molecular structure. This kind of temperamental affinity, with large issues and realms, is well-documented – but there is another, and I suspect it is far more common than the other. This is the affinity for a smaller place where the scientists feels at home. Some whom we think of primarily as biologists or naturalists work from this affinity, this love of place, and in this love find inspiration and clarity of vision. I think of Art Flick, not a professional entomologist, mostly a fisherman, guide and fly tier, whose love of the Schoharie River in the Catskill Mountains of New York was such that virtually all of his significant work on insects (work which has been terribly important for anglers and entomologists alike) was done on that single stream. His collecting and observing, his seeing, made available information which has proven significant anywhere aquatic insects live. But Flick's home, his laboratory, his love was the Schoharie. To have found such a place, and to be able to begin looking there, gives one a tremendous advantage on the path to seeing nature.

My advice is: do not hope to be a Darwin, to want to make global connections, to travel everywhere searching for the threads of meaning which unite the natural world. Such wide-ranging observation seems for the most part to benefit me little, and the seeing of connections in that context will surely escape me. I do much better, having found a home, when I look closely at the things around me. Perhaps, with the gradual accumulation of observations at home, and the seeing of the many connections which are immediately before us waiting to be perceived, we equip ourselves with the tools necessary for wider, more ambitious journeys. Maybe this is where even a Darwin starts, or perhaps this is just *my* temperament. In either case, it is an approach which I find comfortable, and one which I feel comfortable recommending as well.

There is a scale to observation which parallels the scale of time. This is one of the great joys of seeing nature, of learning to see more clearly. It is a short step from the observation of local weather to a consideration of continental effects, the position of distant seas and mountains. Observation of migrating animals immediately raises questions about the lands which the animals who move through our lives and places inhabit when they are not present. The water which flows in our streams and rivers either goes from our homes to a very different and distant place, or comes to us from such a place, or perhaps both. The global interrelatedness of natural events is unavoidable. Having seen clearly the presence of such things in the place we know best, we begin to understand the other places as well. It is exhilarating to become lost in the magnitude of natural events, but somehow special to be at home with those we experience daily. If someone were to ask me, "Where should I look to begin to see nature?," I think I would have to answer, "Begin by going home and looking under your feet."

III. The Eyes of Our Species

THERE EXISTS IN the seeing of nature, in any seeing, a delicate balance between the chaos of ignorance, with its gift of freshness, and the order of knowledge, with its curse of restricted vision. All attempts to understand seeing involve, to some extent, the discussion of order and chaos, with their associated gifts and evils.

If there were no benefit to learning, to the ordering of experience, then there would be no need to look in the first place; all that is good and useful would come with us into the world. If there were no curse in the accumulation of knowledge, then we would not have the fact of experienced eyes sometimes failing to see the obvious. When freshness of vision is balanced with breadth of experience, truly amazing things are seen.

It is normal to perceive order in the natural world, and anyone who has spent time looking finds the argument about whether order inheres in the world or in our perception of it spurious. We have learned that the sun returns each day, bringing warmth and light; that the earth revolves around the sun, bringing the rhythms of seasons, of plant and animal growth, times of germination, birth and development, which fit into those seasons as comfortably as a seed blown by the wind fits into the furrow which finally becomes its home. We have learned to see rhythm in the coming and going of game through our places of habitation, in patterns and cycles of weather, in the many events which constitute the natural world. We have learned to see ourselves as a part of these rhythms, as natural. Surely this learning has been good, and useful. Through it we have found food, shelter and the means for survival, and after these needs had been met, we came to find something more in it: the pleasure of understanding. It has been argued that the history of man's discovery of repetitive rhythms in nature, a series of discoveries which contain the record of our survival and development as a species, also mirrors our perceptions of beauty: the things we call beautiful somehow contain references to an unconscious awareness of rhythm and its necessity in our growth as a species.

How then can learning, the discovery of order in chaos, be considered somehow bad? Why do we long for the innocent vision of youth, for the chaos of ignorance? If learning represents the perception of rhythm, the basis of beauty, the very soul of survival, why should anyone wish to replace it with something else? How can something as vague as *freshness* ever hope to replace what our accumulated knowledge has already given us? The answer is that there is learning, and there is Learning. In the difference, difficult to discern, lies a clue to the difference between looking and seeing.

Perhaps it would prove illuminating to look for answers about the conflict between order and chaos, between knowledge and freshness in the kinds of perceptions we have held about nature. Where do we look to find clues about the way man has seen nature? One place is in the historical record which exists in our aesthetic artifacts. Perhaps the most significant fact which emerges from an examination of the arts is the existence of recurrent themes and

ON SEEING NATURE

trends, themes which indicate something deeper than personal idiosyncrasy. In the arts we see strong evidence for the belief that some of our responses are species-wide, and not specific to individuals.

In the 18th century there emerged a system of classification in the visual arts. This system included the notions of the beautiful, the sublime and the picturesque. While these notions proved extremely useful for the classification of art objects relating to nature, their utility transcends this task.

The categories were based on responses to collections of visual data, or more simply put, to the ways we might describe *scenes*. Some scenes were said to be beautiful, others sublime, and still others picturesque. I suspect that these terms were in common usage before anyone tried to nail down their meaning, but an attempt to do just that was made, and here are the conclusions:

The beautiful was said to depend on a sense of nurturing and well-being. Beauty presupposed safety, was seen as pleasing and gentle, and was said to inspire the instinct of self-propagation.

The sublime, on the other hand, was perceived as threatening. Sublimity presupposes massive scale, vastness, power and great strength, or overwhelming solitude. One's response to the sublime was fear. One's immediate goal, to find shelter and safety. Self-preservation was the instinct thought to have been stimulated.

The notion of the picturesque, which emerged somewhat later, is based on a response which is pleasant, to scenes which are familiar. We see it in places and images

which contain the clues of historic continuity, domestication of nature, and evidence of the presence of man in the landscape. The picturesque emerges from the sublime at the precise point where the rural emerges from the wild. The picturesque, involving familiarity, historic continuity and man fitting comfortably into his surroundings, is often said to stimulate the intellectualization of our visual relationship with nature.

What do all of these constructs have in common? Well, for one thing, they assume that order can be forged from the complexity of nature and given a name. This is a very human trait, and a significant one in any examination of the problem of seeing nature. More important, though, is the realization that, with these categories, thousands of years of art can be examined and a simple and wonderful conclusion drawn: we have responded to nature in similar fashion for a long, long time. We have seen not only with the eyes of individuals, but with the eyes of our species.

Our art history is more than a record of the objects we call art. It is in a very basic sense a record of what we are, and how we see; and its language, the visual products and the words of criticism, contains significant clues about our biological heritage.

If we are to truly see nature we must somehow escape the limitations of our experience and claim an understanding which transcends individual perception. Is there in our visual history substantiation for the belief that a mechanism for this escape from personal limitation exists; that there might be truth in the thought that consciousness of the natural world, the seeing of nature, includes elements we bring with us into life – elements which unite our experience and our perception, our seeing, with those of our ancestors? If we think of ourselves as biological/genetic entities, the thought is not so terribly radical or extreme. When we see ourselves as part of nature, in the same way that other creatures are part of nature, the conclusion is obvious. We transcend our personal limitations through the same mechanism that other organisms use: our genetic foundation, the information in our cells which carries the lessons of previous successes and has lost the worst of our failures. We live and procreate thanks to this heritage. We see with it as well.

It is not difficult to imagine the scenario under which our responses to places, and then pictures of places, came to include such things as fear and pleasure. We can imagine the visual development of mankind progressing much as the visual development of an individual progresses. In a beginning which is too distant to describe with complete accuracy, it seems appropriate to imagine that situations were mostly perceived as neutral. With the passage of time, the coming and going of generations, survival may have favored those who could sense danger before it was too late, or find safety and comfort (and therefore needed rest), without coming to grief because of an erroneous perception. Is it possible that the process of selection has genetically preserved the ability to see such things in the environment? Perhaps we have even developed to the point of sensing safety and pleasure, or danger and fear in visual representations of nature, without fully understanding the basis of

these perceptions in our genetic history. It was John Dewey who argued that all discussions of the beautiful may be framed in the language of historical, genetic, human development, a development which finds order and rhythm in nature, and therefore beauty in its direct and indirect representations. The biologist Edmund O. Wilson expanded the argument to include the thought that there is a universally accepted image of the ideal home and its setting (the picturesque?) which has as its source the environment in which early man found safety, shelter, food and water. Both maintain that some learning, learning which has proven adaptive through millennia and not just a few centuries or decades, has the capacity to be transmitted genetically. We have developed the notions, whether we can articulate them or not, of the beautiful, the sublime and the picturesque as a result of our historical interaction with nature, and we have transmitted these notions genetically, across the barriers of time and culture. It would not be terribly brash to conclude that other notions have been transmitted as well. Certainly this learning and its contents constitute a part of the Learning we need in order to see nature.

Along with our development of the ability to perceive inherent safety and danger, we have developed institutions which help mediate between us and the dangers to our survival which exist in the natural world. Few of us hunt for food, and risk losing our lives in the process. Few of us explore new territory to follow game, or live in the outdoors risking exposure to the elements. The degree to which we require acute perceptions of danger (and can thereby fully appreciate safety and beauty) has been reduced. Our natural ability to perceive, to see, has been diluted by the development of our varied cultural institutions, and, broadly, by the march of civilization. In order to recapture the acute perception we possess as a result of our genetic heritage, it is necessary to remove ourselves from the protection of cultural institutions every now and then, to face naked the fact of a broader natural world.

Experiences of awe in nature, times when we are alone with our fears and the massive scale of the natural world, are good for us, and beneficial to the process of seeing. Being on a beach while storm winds howl and waves crash; sitting out a thunderstorm in an exposed place, coming upon a great chasm or massive peak unexpectedly – all of these put us in touch with our ability to see nature. To expose oneself to unnecessary risk cannot be said to be adaptive, but to have found oneself exposed, to have survived through wits and perhaps a little luck, especially in the face of something huge and powerful, enriches one's life and one's perceptions. Never to have experienced such risk or natural power diminishes our lives and our perceptions.

There have been many times when I have experienced awe in the face of nature, sensing the source of my awareness of the sublime, but one event looms nearly as large in memory as the element of nature which caused it.

Once, when I was younger, less experienced and more foolish than I am today, I found myself in the company of two others on a mountain climb. It was a mountain I had looked at for years and always wanted to climb. The massive summit looms over the region in which I live, and is visible from nearly every peak I have ever been on. My partners were both experienced climbers, and the time seemed right for an attempt. I had done a little canyon climbing with one of the members of our party, and while I had never been out with the other, I had heard great things about his previous climbs and believed him to have a good deal of experience. I knew that my skills were limited, but thought that the greater experience of this new member of our party would compensate for my limitations. The very steep climb was to involve a good deal of snow, and perhaps some ice. I had done a little practicing on some easier routes in preparation for this climb, and now that we were on the mountain, slowly moving upward, I was full of joy and expectation.

We had spent the previous night sleeping on the ground at the base of the mountain at an elevation of about 8,000 feet, and we were climbing slowly, unroped, up a steep scree slope which lay at the foot of the eastern buttress of the over 14,000-foot peak we hoped to climb. Our bones and muscles ached from the cold night and the hard ground, but the weight of our climbing packs filled with gear, the steady uphill rhythm, the sweat and the heat generated in the effort soon worked out the kinks. We began to flow up the mountain. I remember a great feeling of confidence coming over me as we moved steadily upward. The valley floor receded, peaks in the distance began to rise up from the horizon as the scene changed from the green of the forests at the valley floor to the gray, brown and white of a rocky slope above timberline. The scree gave way to boulders, and then to rock walls. We continued to climb, and still felt no need of the ropes. Above us loomed the summit, a jagged, massive pinnacle of rock, surprisingly devoid of the snow and ice our distant views had led us to expect. The route appeared obvious, and almost disappointingly simple. We wondered why we had filled our packs with the heavy gear we thought we would need. Too many ropes, too much hardware, extra clothing and ice axes – they seemed so unnecessary (and they were getting heavy). We made extraordinarily good time, and when we paused for lunch, the summit, though still looming over us above the ridge at the top of the buttress we climbed, seemed even smaller and more manageable. Along with the cheese and sardines, crackers, lemonade and water, we passed kidding remarks and jokes. The sun was warm, and our spirits high.

After lunch we continued to climb. Our progress indicated that we would gain the ridge at the top of the buttress in early afternoon, and then need a few hours for the final push to the summit. Time was on our side.

As we came over the ridge, filled with joy, we saw it – rising up above us, across a deep dark chasm, rose a tremendous snow, ice and rock wall. It grew larger with every step toward the ridge top. Finally, on the ridge, we stared in silence. The summit of the mountain we were climbing was not the pinnacle of rock we had been eyeing all day; that was merely a large gendarme on a minor ridge. The spot on which we now stood lay at the base of this pinnacle. Across the gulf which separated us from the true summit loomed the mountain we had come to ascend. Its face dove down nearly 500 feet below us, and its summit towered over us, several thousand feet higher than the high buttress we had spent seven hours climbing. Its face was dark. It looked bitterly cold. It was huge. And it frightened the hell out of me.

As long as I live I will never forget that moment. No summit or distant peak has looked the same to me since. Without that moment of fear, of awe, of sublime perception, my ability to see would be hopelessly impoverished.

We continued to climb, first down-climbing into the valley beneath the peak, and then up a steep snow gully that lay at the base of the face. As we roped up and assembled the gear for snow climbing, I discovered that the climbing partner who was supposed to have the most experience on snow and ice had no more experience than I, and my experience was pitiful. I also discovered that he had been told that I was an experienced snow and ice climber! Both of us were embarrassed when the truth of our inexperience came out on the mountain. The third member of the party was a very strong rock climber, certainly the best among us, but he too was relatively inexperienced on snow and ice. From great confidence, we had fallen to a perception of our-

selves as a weak party. The perception was accurate. The mountain which had seemed so easy a few hours ago, had become the most difficult challenge any of us had yet faced.

We climbed hard, and as fast as we could, but time ran out. We failed to make the summit before dark, and after scouting the face a bit, we retreated rather than spend the night, tired cold and ill-prepared, high on the mountain.

The partners I had that day went back a few years later with two others and successfully climbed the mountain by another route. I know a relatively simple route which lies on the peak's south face, but I have not yet returned to make the summit. The mountain's gift to me that day was a priceless confrontation with the true scale of nature. It was a gift which put me in contact with my own inborn sense of the sublime. I'm not sure I should ask for more.

Beauty is a bit more subtle, perhaps, but no less powerful, and occasionally contemplation of the beautiful leads directly to perceptions of the sublime. The reverse is also true. What characterizes beauty, perhaps more than any other category of perception, is an association with order and a sense of well-being. This contrasts sharply with our perception of the sublime. There is certainly order in the sublime, but no sense of well-being. Once we begin to feel comfortable, we move into the realm of the beautiful.

The concept of beauty, unfortunately, has been asked to carry a heavy load; we have required that it be the bearer of the unbearable. The notion has been torn apart in the analysis we call philosophical inquiry. Historically, beauty has

been the construct under which we have debated the question of the existence of art, and whether or not an object should be called art. To a large extent the history of aesthetics is the history of our concept of beauty. Recently the attention of aestheticians has, fortunately, shifted somewhat. Now, when we choose to be philosophical about art, we argue about the use of language, and about expression, the nature of emotional content and how it is communicated. Beauty is a little bit neglected, but that allows us to talk about it without getting bogged down in questions of formal aesthetics. Beauty in nature, and in representations of nature, is not a measure of the goodness of something. It does not involve a ranking by relative merit. Things are not more or less beautiful (just as representations of nature are not legitimately judged to be either art, or not art). The degree to which we *see* the beautiful in nature, or in anything else for that matter, is the degree to which we perceive order and rhythm, and associate that with the creative and procreative functions of life. Too simple? Perhaps, but I vastly prefer this approach to one which argues relative merit. Just as with the sublime, the most reliable learning regarding the beautiful that we possess rests in our biological heritage, and, once again, in order to access it, in order to see, we must confront it from time to time as directly as possible, without the intervention of institutional or cultural mediation.

There is a popular method for teaching drawing to artists who want to learn how to render accurately. It is known by various names, but used, in some form, almost universally in art schools and community art workshops. Aspiring artists are given a technique for looking at contours, or for reorienting an object so that it is not recognizable, before they are allowed to draw. People who have never been able to render find, with these devices, that they are able to render with an accuracy that they thought impossible. Such skill, they assumed, was reserved for the supremely gifted. What has happened is that the would-be artist, for the first time perhaps, drew what he or she saw, and not a recreation of an image which was held in the form of an ideal image in their minds. They looked before they drew. If you allow a group of people to draw a tree in nature, without resorting to such pedagogic devices, most will draw the same tree that they would draw in a classroom, without the tree being present. When the object to be drawn is separated from its ideal image, from its name, it is seen as a real object and rendered as such.

Why is the idealized image somehow less reliable than other internal constructs? Well, for one thing, it doesn't very often look like a real tree! More importantly, the contents of these constructs vary with time and culture; like notions of the ideal woman or man, they bear little resemblance to reality. When we look at a tree and see this ideal image, rather than what is actually there, we fail to see. We probably aren't looking very hard either.

Experiences of the beautiful which find their basis in cultural ideals and values have a validity of their own, but

it is not the validity of verisimilitude. In order to experience beauty in a fundamental way it is necessary to confront nature without the blinders of preconception. Our ability to do this lies in the fact that we are creatures who live in nature, and who have done so for millions of years.

The picturesque is a bit more problematic. In searching for the Learning which is reliable, which helps us to see, we have found evidence for the existence of a shared set of perceptions which have developed in our species over a long period of time. These perceptions exist because they have proven adaptive, and, as such, may be considered accurate reflections of the true state of affairs which exists between ourselves as surviving organisms and the environment in which we function. What are we to make of a set of observations of nature which constitutes an historical record of the presence of man in the environment; a set of images and perceptions which is supposed to stimulate the intellectualization of sight; a set which records our dwelling in, and modification of, various places? All of this sounds vaguely utilitarian, and perhaps at odds with the accumulated learning of our species. The usefulness of the beautiful and the sublime lies, to a large extent, in the lack of intellectual interaction with places and things. It lies in the gift of immediate perception, of feeling – and of intellectualization only later, and perhaps as a dilution of the true perception. The picturesque, as defined art-historically, presupposes intellectualization. Is this all there is to it?

In the 18th century the analysis of art (within our own European tradition) was undertaken as an expression of fondness for human products. Art was seen, and still is by many, as another demonstration of human superiority and dominance over mere nature. As such, renderings of nature which were beautiful, and those which were sublime, were evaluated in terms of the thoughts such renderings might generate, and not with the kind of language we have been using. A genetic heritage of adaptive perceptions which united mankind with other organisms was not perceived by many, and there is little record of its having been discussed by serious critics. Man's ability to render the beautiful and the sublime was mistaken as a talent which separated him from the rest of nature, which made him somehow better than the rest of the natural world. In their analysis of the picturesque, critics carried this conclusion to extremes. In the picturesque we glorified the domination of nature by man, not the recognition of our place within it.

I would be caught in the most hideous inconsistency, however, if I were to hold that the presence of the beautiful and sublime in our art through time and in divergent cultures indicates a valuable kind of species-wide learning, while the presence of the picturesque does not. What is there to learn from our innate sense of the picturesque?

The value of the picturesque lies not in the specific details which render the picturesque for isolated cultural groups. That there are tulips predominating in some paintings of gardens, and roses in others, is not relevant, except as an indication of cultural preference. In some paintings

the picturesque involves thatched roofs and narrow, over-grown country lanes, while in others it is represented by slate roofs and wide avenues where vegetation has been kept at bay. What is common to all renderings of the pictur-esque is the notion of imprint, the idea that man, as an agent acting within nature, has the power to create for him-self a niche, a home. To value this concept is not to elevate man above other species, but to create a basis for the recog-nition of the same urge in other creatures. And to respect it. When this tendency is recognized in its various forms throughout much of the natural world, our seeing of suita-ble habitats (those of our own species, and of others) and of the dwellings within them is increased. Our desire to reck-lessly modify nature is mitigated, and our ability to per-ceive the countless modifications wrought by others is en-hanced. We walk a fine line here between seeing and pro-jection, but freed from the curse of anthropocentrism, it is my hope that the line can be walked successfully, and the result is more clarity of vision.

In thinking about the beautiful, the sublime and the pic-turesque, we have certainly not covered all of the terrain which exists regarding species-wide knowledge. Hopefully, what we have discovered is that such knowledge exists. If we want to find out what learning aids in the seeing of na-ture, this shared vision is a good place to start our search. The more we make use of this knowledge, the more clearly we see. In order to maximize those experiences in which we see with the eyes of our species, we must confront na-ture with fresh eyes, accepting the chaos of confusion at first, attempting to see what is really there and not what we have been led to expect.

Where does this leave science, the naturalist's great ally, and the rubric under which much serious observation of nature seems to fall? On firmer ground, I hope.

There is a great deal to be learned from the natural sciences. Major leaps of vision occur when the observations of many are organized into coherent systems of thought. Indeed, much of what I have said regarding the transmission of species-wide knowledge assumes the acceptance of certain scientific values and systems. Without the notion of natural selection, the meaning of adaptive behavior would make no sense. The idea that such recurring tendencies can be transmitted rests on the assumption that genetic material exists, and that it carries information from the cells of the progenitor to those of the progeny. What is this if not science? We must exercise caution, however. That great leaps in knowledge occur in the sharing of observations and in the formation of systems is obvious. That we also share and perpetuate some horrendous mistakes is not so widely acknowledged. While the limits and contents of shared *enduring* knowledge are not known to me, I believe them to be reliable (even if current theories about their roots in adaptation and genetic transmission were to be proven false). Natural science is an incredibly powerful tool, but its conclusions must always be considered tentative. Its internal tests involve matters of logical consistency, the ability to contain observed phenomena, predictive accuracy, and an ethereal thing called elegance. The external test of science involves consistency, with the rather imprecise area of species-wide knowledge, in its relation to our collective wisdom. For the most part, we see better when we have access to the observations of others, and to the ordering of these observations in the systems represented in natural science; we must remember, however, that science has its limits, that there is a danger in the creation of names and the development of systems. That danger is the assumption of familiarity, sometimes, where no true familiarity dwells.

There exists in the natural sciences a marvelous tradition; it is the tradition of the amateur scientist. For those who would see nature, this is a wonderful tradition within which to function. Amateur astronomers routinely observe things which had not been noticed by professionals. Amateur ornithologists perform the lion's share of the work involved with observing bird movement and recording changes in populations due to changes in habitat and the introduction of toxins into the environment. One need not devote one's life to the pursuit of natural science in order to participate, or to learn; and the level and form ones's participation takes is based solely on one's interests and desires. The most important aspect of amateur naturalism, however, is that it involves us firsthand in the business of looking. There is an incredible difference between reading about species in a book, or studying descriptions of ecosystems, and trying to find those species in the field, or observing firsthand the collections of beings that live together. In this disciplined looking we build upon our innate association with the natural world, and if we keep our eyes open, we might just find a few things that were left out of our books. Best of all, this wonderful pastime requires no money, no travel and no need to radically alter our lives. We begin with our own backyards, with the sky over our heads and the earth at our feet.

Where I have chosen to live there are mountains. I came here because I was attracted to the grand gesture, to the massive scale of the place, to the sense of awe I felt here as nowhere else. Now that I have been here awhile, I find that the size, the awesomeness, have become less significant to me, and I am able to see details that I missed before. My interests have grown, and my attention has shifted somewhat. These changes are reflected in the way I spend my time, and in the ways I choose to pursue my own limited amateur naturalism.

The sky over my head is rimmed with high mountains, but the earth at my feet, the space between the peaks, is filled with running water. That water is filled with life. A major preoccupation of mine (a malady perhaps) is fishing. Not just fishing, but fishing for trout. Not just fishing for trout, but fishing for trout with an artificial fly. Out of this malady, a group of associated interests has developed. These include a love of the literature that this ancient pastime has spawned, for aquatic entomology and the study of trout habitats, for the making of imitations of insects with feathers and fur, and for observing the behavior of trout and the things they eat. If ever the tremendous power of science to clarify vision were made obvious, it is in its application to the problem of fooling a trout with an artificial fly.

Unfortunately, every day I am reminded of its limitations as well, of the need to see what is really happening, and not to be misled by expectations.

The literature of angling, half science, half poetry, has given me eyes I would not have had if I'd never been exposed to it. The life cycles of aquatic insects, the habitats in which they live, the minor deviations in stream bottom and water flow that make the difference between finding fish who will likely feed, and those who are hiding from predators – these and a million other topics are covered and shared in the literature. To learn these things exclusively through personal observation would require an enormous amount of time. Learning from the experiences of others gives us a significant advantage. It allows us to greatly expand the amount of legitimate learning we may acquire in our lifetimes. Such learning is not a substitute for personal experience, however, and is largely worthless without it. Our own backyards, the places that interest us most, are likely to be significantly different from the simplified, generalized descriptions we read in literature, or even in scientific texts. The real learning begins when we sift our own dirt through our own fingers, when we stalk our own creatures, when we stand knee-deep in the tugging currents of our own streams, when we sniff our own air. I can recall many examples of conflicting information in the literature of trout, conflicts which were continued and debated for years, until someone observed that the discrepancy lay in the difference between the home streams of the disagreeing authors, in the fact that they each had made valid observations for their own place and time – observations, however, which could not be generalized. To expand our vision of nature, to see her more clearly, we do well to read as much natural science as we find interesting. For some this will be a great deal. For others it will be considerably less, and for these there will be a lot of time spent reinventing the wheel. While this may not be terribly efficient, who cares? What we are talking about is a personal relationship with the natural world, a labor of love, an individual desire to see, not a race with prizes for the winners and disgrace for the losers. Considering all that there is to see, and all that we remain ignorant about, both the wisest and the most ignorant of us know relatively little. Any prizes are personal. So must be the route taken to vision.

Ideally, science provides a tentative framework for observation, and expands significantly our visual abilities. Too often, however, we are blinded by the seeming power of applying the observations of others; fail to make our own, and therefore fail to see what is in front of our noses. If I were to go to a new place, and have access to a scientist who was not familiar with the place, and an astute observer who lived in the place but had read little science, I believe I would choose the latter as my guide. Besides being less likely to get lost, and probably seeing more country, I think I'd learn more.

We sit on a fence, straddling the pitfalls of chaos and order, between ignorance and knowledge. While knowledge
would seem to be the better choice, its dangers are as real as
those of chaos. In chaos we have observations, but no way
to make sense of them. With order we have categories of
thought in which to file observations, but find that these
critical observations have been tainted by our categories.
Fortunately, we have our wonder to sustain interest, and
the eyes of our species to provide wisdom. Learning which
progresses from this base is capable of tolerating a certain
amount of chaos, is able to temper the bias of culture; it expands our ability to observe, and brings us closer to the natural world we wish to see.

IV. The Habit of Metaphor

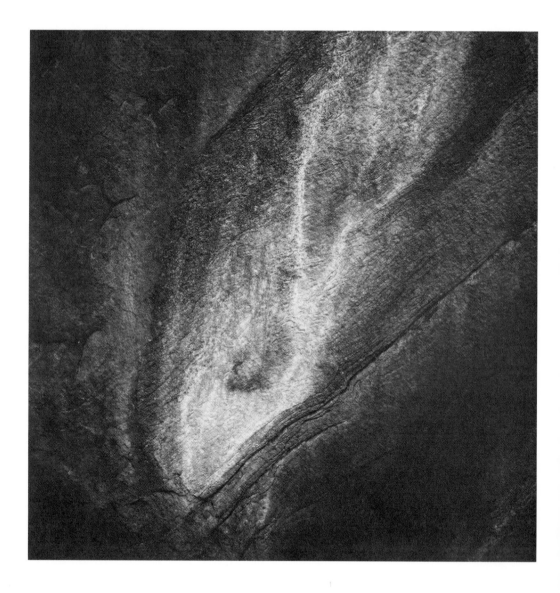

THE DESIRE TO *see* nature, to transcend mundane vision, is, in the last analysis not a desire to see more, but to see differently. For us, as adults, this means somehow escaping the categories of thought which limit our perception.

In science we have often noticed a kind of shared vision which limits perception, and also the periodic revolutionary perceptions which alter that vision forever. At any given time we are likely to grasp the current shared image of reality and hold on as if to a life raft, asserting that it represents truth. It is helpful to remember that the same fervor existed in defense of the images which have been discarded, and lie in ruin, the dusty historical relics of a misguided past. For centuries Newton was believed to have seen and articulated the mind of God, to have quantified His laws, to have described nature. The clockwork mechanism which emerged, the regulated universe which arose out of universal gravitation, disappeared as the clock became individual clocks, each distorted, as if in a Dali painting, by the local effects of a newly postulated general relativity. Time itself became irregular, and, when linked with space in the reality fabric of space-time, became a partner in the destruction of our notion of fixed length, and mass. Now the very concept of certainty through scientific questioning has been abandoned, and an epistemology which promised to replace metaphysics begins to look more like metaphysics than anything else.

The desire to see nature, through science as through poetry, has become an exploration of metaphor, and it is with metaphor that one must become comfortable if one wishes to see.

There are many exercises which are used to encourage the habit of metaphorical perception. Often they are drawn from the experiences of others. When such exercises are shared, they allow us to learn to see by imitating the things others have done. More important than the performing of exercises, perhaps, is an awakening to our own special perceptions, and the realization that they are precious, and valid, no matter how strange they may sometimes appear.

Take the roundness of the earth, for example. We have learned that the earth is round. We have heard it said so often, in so many different ways, that we no longer find the idea strange. Only a very few years ago the idea had to be taken on faith. It was an inference from indirect observation. I remember sitting as a child on the beach, looking eastward out over the sea toward the horizon, trying to see, to feel in the pit of my stomach the roundness of the earth. Sometimes much time would pass, and I would just sit. The waves would become a hissing in consciousness, and the rest of the scene would disappear as the sea and the horizon grew to become everything. The sun would climb in the sky. Sometimes ships would emerge from the sea, climbing the horizon, or they would slowly sink from view sailing over it. At some point the roundness of the earth ceased to be an idea that I had been taught; it became a very real and powerful perception. I would feel myself rolling with the earth. The sun, stationary in the firmament, would sit above me as I rolled with the earth's surface under it. Now, as often as I can, in various places, I repeat this experience (I especially like to do it in the desert). I sit still until I can feel the earth rolling. To have experienced the roundness of the earth is, I think, a very important thing, and something everyone, should experience.

The importance of the experience, of directly perceiving the fact of the earth's roundness and not simply taking it as an article of faith, is that the experience contradicts ordinary perception. It is good to know that the true nature of nature sometimes does contradict our immediate impressions, and, with something as powerful and grand as a perception of the roundness of the earth it is a lesson we do not soon forget.

Euclid systematized a useful and magnificently elegant mathematical technique which we know as plane geometry. That this technique also represented an image of nature and the earth's surface is sometimes forgotten now that we have become sophisticated in our awareness of spherical and other geometries. That it was useful cannot be denied. That it accurately represented the state of affairs on an isolated segment of the earth's surface can be. When the segment becomes larger, the fundamental limitations of Euclidean space become apparent. Surveyors start to see the effects of curvature as they attempt to extend straight lines over longer distances. For them, a perception of the rolling earth, direct knowledge of the roundness of our planet, comes with time in the field. Euclid's geometry (and Newton's physics, for that matter) ceases to be considered a true representation of nature within a limited arena, and becomes a sometimes useful tool and extraordinarily beautiful mathematical triumph not necessarily connected with the real world. The fact of the earth, the experience of it, overwhelms intellectual categories. It is the fact of the earth, of nature, we must experience in order to see.

In the early days of the space program much of the information, including photographs, was kept classified by the government. There were some who argued that a release of these images would forever alter our perceptions of ourselves and of nature. It would be easy to destroy a planet if one did not sense its fragility and isolation in space, if one could not see directly the fact of its self-contained and self-dependent nature. (Remember the Whole Earth Society, which pushed for the release of images of the earth, in its totality, floating in the vacuum of space?). When, finally, those images were released, when we were able to see the incredible beauty of the blue globe of the earth, its white turbulence, the weather systems of its atmosphere, the visual evidence of creative and destructive forces moving around its surface, when we saw for the first time the deep blackness of that which surrounds it, we sensed directly, and probably for the first time, our incredibly profound isolation, and the special fact of our being here. This perception, not so terribly distant for most of us, and not so terribly common that it has lost its power, is a representation of the kinds of seeing we must court if we are to grow in our seeing of nature.

Although the earth would appear to be flat, we know it to be round, and in some cases we have been able to transcend the limitation of narrow vision and actually perceive this roundness directly. A similar kind of potential error in seeing exists in our perception of the stability and unchanging nature of the earth's surface. Most of us possess a basic understanding of geological process, but few of us have any gut feeling for the changes which occur constantly, for the flow which exists in the rock, seemingly solid, which surrounds us. An immediate sense of the roundness of the earth is a wonderfully liberating perception. So is a direct experience of the flux which constitutes the state of the earth's surface. Many of us can perceive the flowing, slow though it may be, of a glacier. Glaciers look somewhat like streams, and we find the metaphor of flowing water easily transferred to ice over rock. Ice falls become rapids, crevasses riffles, and broad flows the glides and deeps of flowing rivers. How many of us can transfer this metaphor to stone? How many of us see the eroding and rebounding, the uplift, the sedimentation, the folding and fracturing as a fluid process of constant change? How many of us can put this in temporal perspective, can see our lives, the evolution and existence of man as a rapidly formed and rapidly to-be-burst bubble in the turbulent stream of geological time?

A technique exists for seeing rock flow like water, and while it can be explained with the constructs of the physiology and psychology of vision, and therefore reduced to meaninglessness, I am convinced that having seen solid rock flow, one never sees rock quite the same again. It is called the Aristotle effect.

If you sit by a waterfall (the longer the free fall of the water the better) and concentrate on a single particle of falling water, watching it pass through the air from the lip of the fall to the stream it joins at the fall's bottom, near where you are sitting; if you can repeatedly transfer your attention from one particle of water to another, from top to bottom, following the flow, over and over, until the meaning of water, and falling, of up and down, have become confused; if you work hard to concentrate on each piece of water as you watch it fall from the top to the bottom, and gazing back up follow another, and still another; if after doing this for several minutes you suddenly transfer your gaze to the supposed solidity and fixedness of the ground on which you sit – an amazing thing will be seen. The ground will appear to flow. It will flow like the water at which you have been gazing.

The first time I did this I was frightened, and I felt nausea. Not a small part of this nausea was due to the feeling that the earth upon which I sat had ceased to be reliable, that it flowed unexpectedly and unpredictably. As the illusion passed and the ground became stable, the nausea and fear disappeared. Reflection, however, has sustained the perception of the movement and changing nature of the earth's surface, of the slow but real motion of stone, and this experience coupled with others has led to a much more immediate perception of geological process, and therefore of time, of permanence, and of impermanence.

All of this translation from one experience, of an immediate nature, to a perception of tremendous scope – from seeing the horizon at the sea and watching the sun rise and fall, to the roundness and rolling of the earth; from flowing water and the illusion of flowing rock, to the movement and change of the earth's surface – seems quite inexact and unreliable. As is already quite evident, I am attracted to notions which have long been around, to behaviors which seem to indicate something fundamental and genetically preserved, in our species. This tendency to reason from metaphor, to presume to know what reason might tell us we cannot know, is such a trait. We see it in our stories and legends, in our great myths. We see it in the most revered activities we pursue, in our music and art, in our literature and in science. The tendency to create knowledge of that which is great, out of experiences with the immediate and small, has been with us for a long time and has resulted in a great many deeply moving human products. For want of a better name, I will call this tradition, this way of working and seeing, that of the Microcosm and the Macrocosm. It appears in literature as seemingly diverse as Goethe and Vonnegut, and in activities generally presumed to have little in common, like science and poetry. Yet, the metaphorical representations of poetry, the play of language, is not so terribly different from the thought experiments which gave us relativity. The tendency is universal, and perhaps more important, not only is it useful but it results in a most real and meaningful kind of pleasure – the pleasure of vision.

Applied in the woods, in an attempt to see nature, it loses none of that ability to give pleasure, and none of its usefulness. All climbers are aware of the difficulty of finding routes on large walls of rock, and I doubt there is one who did not learn to deal with this difficulty by first finding routes in miniature on small boulders. Many I know expand the exercise farther, finding routes on pebbles, and seeing them as mountains. After doing this for a while, it is not difficult to imagine a pebble as a mountain, to be overwhelmed with the complexity and beauty, the grandeur of a tiny stone. What began as an exercise to reduce the complexity of a mountain, an exercise which succeeds in that goal handily, has become something else, something more, something metaphorical and not utilitarian. Instead of the mountain becoming a manageable boulder, the pebble has become an unmanageable mountain. The mountain and the pebble have become one. The microcosm has been connected with the macrocosm through metaphor, and our perception has become enriched in the process.

A similar technique is used by whitewater canoeists, kyakers and rafters to learn to read water, and the results are the same. Big water is incredibly confusing at first. Holes which can be life-taking are hard to differentiate from eddies which can be life-saving. Tongues, standing waves, rips, spray, pillows and rocks appear as utter chaos. Looking at rapids in miniature, finding the same hydraulics in a stream, allows the beginner to make sense out of the cacophony, to build music from disparate sound, or more accurately, to see the symphony which exists but overwhelms in the first encounters. Given time, and the temperament, it is possible to see the turbulence in a trickle, the grand river in the passage of rainwater over the surface of the ground: to perceive directly, and not through inference, the intimate relationship which exists between atmospheric water, rain, and the mighty rivers which roar over the surface of our earth.

In this tradition of the microcosm and the macrocosm, firmly seated at its center, sits the child on a hill, at night, gazing at the stars, seeing in their great distance, in their incredible profusion, his own smallness. There sits a child who moves from that smallness to a feeling of connectedness, and a size much greater than a diminutive child's stature. The child who has carried this wonder, this seeing of the microcosm and the macrocosm into adulthood, is the adult who sees stars in the spots on the skin of a sugar-rich apple, the firmament in its spherical surface, the cosmos in the lichen which populate the surface of a rock, the adult who continues to look at the night sky and see much more than stars.

How many of us as children, with a primitive understanding of solar systems and atoms, speculated on the repetitive form of nature as we moved through size and orders of magnitude? How many of us wondered if solar systems might be the atoms of still larger galaxies, and galaxies of still larger universes, if universes themselves might not be mere atoms in something larger? How many of us wondered at what size, at what unimaginable limit of scale the progression had to stop, and God Himself had to be invented to halt the process? How many of us stopped thinking such things when we nailed down, or thought we had, the differences between atoms and solar systems? How many of us contracted our thought with the adoption of simplistic theisms? How many of us had our vision impoverished by this kind of learning? How many of us are willing (as yet another expression of the metaphor of the microcosm and the macrocosm emerges) to regress into this childlike thought in order to progress in our vision?

The metaphor, then, is not simply a figure of speech. It is a habit of thought, one we must develop in order to see. The habit of metaphor allows us to see the large from the small, the pattern in chaos, that which is not expected, that which *is* expected, in new ways. Metaphor allows us to see with eyes expanded beyond the simply literal, the cataloging of perceptions. Metaphor allows us to see relationships. Ultimately, it is relationships which constitute nature, not collections of individual objects.

One of the great joys of living in the mountains is the ease with which one may move through the seasons, through climatic zones, through plant and animal communities. It is possible to eat one's breakfast at home, basking in the warmth of the summer sun, grab one's pack and begin walking in the life zone known as the Montane, amble upward, as summer retreats into spring through the retreating snows of the Hudsonian, and finally, don parka and skis to meet winter in the arctic world of the alpine tundra. On hikes of this nature with visitors, I often hear comments such as these from those who are new to this special environment. "What are these doing here? These

ON SEEING NATURE

trees are so small, and they haven't even shown their buds yet? Don't they know its July?" Well, it may be July, but in the Hudsonian, spring is just coming, and up higher, it is definitely winter. When your mind tells you that it must be summer because the calendar says July, you may miss a few things, but if you can move into spring, and then winter, whatever the calendar says, you have begun to acquire the habit of metaphor. Even more common than any surprise at the change of seasons with altitude, is the difficulty some people have believing that they need to prepare for winter when assembling a pack for a mountain hike. It is hard to deny evidence which is staring you in the face (though some try hard to do just that), but imagining in the absence of evidence is even harder. More than once I've had people become annoyed with me, when after listening to their reasons for not wanting to carry warm clothing, I say, "You have to remember, it's still winter there." Some people don't like to have their calendars rearranged.

To make matters worse, elevation is not the only factor influencing the flow of seasons. Often in mid-winter, at high altitude (where it is often winter during the summer), there exist pockets of spring! Microclimates exist everywhere, but nowhere have they been as obvious to me as in the mountains. Sometimes, in a nook on a south-facing slope – perhaps in a hollow surrounded by dark stone, sheltered from wind, warmed by the sun and the heat-retaining properties of the rock – a springlike bud, or even bloom, will appear in the winter. Try hiking with someone who was annoyed last summer when you kept telling them to remember that it was "winter up there," and now tell them "it's spring in there!" This sort of thing usually gets me a snowball (which I dodge) and a chuckle (which I love). The chuckle means that my companion has gone from calendars to metaphor, from the literal to the real. Try telling someone who is uncomfortable with a rearranged calendar that there is a difference between the literal and the real, and see what *that* gets you. Might be more than a snowball.

Microclimates, like zone and climatic changes with elevation, are surprises when seen with literal eyes, eyes with limited expectations. The seeing, and the understanding of microclimates is important. To see them, one must understand the notion of pattern, and then having seen a pattern, one must see a deviation, and then having seen the deviation, one must detect a smaller pattern. Finally, if one sees really well, the microclimate and the surrounding pattern become related, and the integration of nature as a whole emerges. It starts with microclimates.

There are many manifestations of the microclimate; the budding plant at high altitude in the middle of winter - exists within one. The wall of moss and ferns, dripping water, which is surrounded by arid country is also one. There are subtle microclimates, like gently raised pieces of ground on which flowers have bloomed while the same plants in the surrounding ground have yet to bloom; and there are blatant microclimates, like oases in the desert. When we see microclimates we make inferences about the conditions which nurture the differences, and in order to do this we must see patterns and not individual events.

One way to amaze friends and influence people is to studiously seek out patterns and microclimates when selecting a campsite. Often, in fact, this becomes a game. Decisions are made in silence, and friends silently compete in a delicate and intriguing game of natural perception. The winner may have a sleeping bag free of ice on a morning when a friend, sleeping not 10 feet away, has found his breathable bag sealed by frost. One tent may be buffeted by winds, while another billows gently through a storm. How do we make these decisions? By looking. By seeing. Can the dominant wind direction be guessed by looking at the slant of grasses, or the deposits of seeds against barriers? Can areas of greater warmth be guessed by looking at the state of development of buds and blooms on similar species? Can gross differences in warmth and wind be inferred from the existence of different plant communities within a small area? Can your eye find ground which is slightly higher (not so much so that it catches wind), around and below which cold air will flow? There is more in this game than simple fun. Developing the ability to solve these riddles, to successfully decipher the subtle mysteries of the microclimate gives a deeper pleasure. It indicates that our senses have not been completely lost in our species' recent fascination with its separateness from nature. For those of us who look for signs that this disease is not terminal, it is an indication of great possibilities. A source of hope. And it will help you get a good night's sleep in the woods.

Metaphor has been thought to be the private realm of the poet and artist. Rather than argue this truth, I choose to believe that seeing, for all of us, involves metaphor. To the extent that we see well, we are all poets and artists.

V. Aesthetic Vision

OBSERVING THAT CHILDREN and adults see differently is relatively easy. Clearly describing the nature of that difference is not so easy. In every child there exist the seeds of future adult perception, and in every adult there are the remains of childhood vision. Still, there are differences.

One way to describe the difference between childlike and less childlike vision is to apply the idea of conservative and non-conservative perception. Often, as we grow older, conservatism becomes a way of life. In some ways this is adaptive, and the result of our growing wisdom. In other ways it is not. Sometimes the conservatism of age deprives us of growth, and locks us into ways of seeing which show little progress and little continued development. Conservatism of this kind is, possibly, the greatest danger and most limiting factor of aging, but such debilitating conservatism is not necessary, and frequently does not occur. How can we avoid the limitations of conservative vision and the stagnation which results? We begin with an understanding of the danger.

The problem of conservative perception is aptly analogized in the metaphor of the pond. Human experience may be thought of as a body of water, each experience perceived being a droplet which adds to the breadth and depth of that body. For the infant, experience is extremely limited, and the puddle which has been created by that experience correspondingly small. Each new experience makes a major contribution to the puddle. Each thing seen, heard, tasted or felt lands on the puddle as a drop which has significant impact. Each experience alters the makeup of the pond. A single drop having a different color or flavor will change the color or flavor of the pond. As we grow older our experiential pond grows until it becomes a lake, and then a vast sea of past experience. New experiences, unless extremely powerful and concentrated, contribute little to the makeup of our sea of experience. Rather than changing the pond, as they did in infancy, the droplets of experience are changed themselves, mixed, diluted, altered, until they are indistinguishable from the body of water into which they have fallen. The color of a new experience disappears, its flavor is diluted. Rather than change the sea, the droplet assumes the color and flavor of the sea into which it has fallen. Experience ceases to have its legitimate impact. The result in vision is that we see not what is before us, but what is inside of us. We fail to see nature. Instead, we project an image of ourselves onto the world, and we ignorantly look at that.

Fortunately this terrible end result is neither universal nor inevitable. Part of the significance of the powerful experience of nature, the seeing of the world from the summit of a high mountain, the experience of lightning crashing nearby, the feeling of being surrounded by the power of a storm, lies in these powerful experiences' ability to alter the makeup of our experiential ponds, no matter how large they have grown. Nature is always larger than our combined experiences. Sometimes we need a bit of a shock to realize that this is the case.

This analogy of the pond also helps explain why going to new places and seeing new things sometimes changes our perceptions of the things we know well, and with which we are most familiar. Totally new experiences do not fit readily into our conceptual seas; they are, in effect, more concentrated experiences, and as such they have more effect on us than experiences which come from places we know. Once our experience has been colored by the new concentrated drops, however, even the familiar takes on a new color.

An attempt to change the nature of our experiential sea seems to characterize much of what we call art. Artists often appear to be looking for the concentrated experience, the distillation of vision which will forever alter the way we see. Some find it, the best communicate it, and after viewing their work we no longer see the world with the same eyes. An attempt to change vision through the presentation of distilled and purified experience seems to be the motivation for much art. The methods which are used to achieve this distillation can help all of us see more clearly.

The search for purified visual experience, and the communication of such experience, seems to determine the way in which many artists work. One common thread which emerges when you speak to artists about their methods is an emphasis on process rather than product, on the making of art and not on the artifacts which result. This emphasis seems to insure that a formula for representing nature will not begin to dominate the work and overpower the real influence of a direct perception of nature. Sometimes, when artists have become successful and their work is expected to look a certain way, formulas, because they have proven commercial value, begin to dominate the art;

but this is not the way artists generally work, and I do not believe it is the way the best work is created.

Often the process assumes the guise of a *problem*, a specific issue or phenomenon on which the artist chooses to isolate attention. The articulation of the problem becomes the framework within which subsequent pieces are made, and through which visual discoveries happen. Usually these self-imposed problems describe rather narrow aspects of reality. Small problems, and their articulation, often seem not only most manageable but most fruitful as well.

This brings us to the issue of abstraction – which relates very directly to all seeing of nature, as well as to the specific act of making representations of what we have seen.

Natural reality exists in a multitude of dimensions beyond the three of length, depth and width. These dimensions of volume fail to describe the dimension of time, which is certainly significant, and in many ways inseparable from volume. Beyond time/space, there are dimensions which come into being because of interactions between objects and creatures who exist in nature. There are smells, feelings of warmth and cold, motion, and associative attributes like danger and safety. The list could grow until it became unmanageable. The point is that any seeing of nature, and any representation of nature, selects limited attributes for attention. All perception, all rendering of nature, involves the act of abstraction. Working artists know this. They know that a painting or photograph is two-dimensional, does not move, has no breath of wind or smell of dirt. In order to create a representation one must either exploit abstraction, magnify it to the point where it is obvious, or deal in illusion, creating a sense of depth and scent, of motion where there is none, by exploiting the ability of abstracted details to imply the presence of these things where they do not exist. In either case, abstraction, the distillation and presentation of a few essential elements of perception, is critical. All perception deals in this kind of abstraction, this inference from selected details. Successful artists manipulate it with conscious intent.

The selection of a *problem* by an artist represents a temporary acceptance of limitations, a set of chosen abstractions, details seen and isolated from nature, with which the artist will work. That acceptance of this limited scope often yields results which teach us a great deal about natural reality and vision beyond the confines of the chosen problem is significant not only for artists, but for all of us. We can all approach nature, at times, in this way. We can select a narrow set of events and examine them in detail, waiting until later to see the connection which exists between this small world we have selected, and the broader one within which it exists.

Seeing in this way is very much like the seeing I discussed earlier as the tradition of the microcosm and the macrocosm, but it is, in some ways, a bit more relaxed. There is no immediate attempt to find cosmic significance in the isolated detail, although this often occurs. It is enough to enjoy the fact of the details, the value of isolated segments in and of themselves.

My own progression as a photographer makes most sense to me when I look at my work and realize that I have photographed with self-imposed restrictions, concentrating on various problems for various amounts of time. The problems have changed with time and place. They seem to have flowed into each other and through my work with a continuity that obscures their presence; but in a wonderful way they have defined my work, allowed the slow growth of insight and vision, and allowed me to see more fully and with greater acuity some of the things which occur in the natural world. I heartily recommend a similar approach to others.

This kind of focus also characterizes much of what we call science, and I believe most of us are familiar with the details of working and seeing in this way, but there are some for whom the approach may sound confusing. An example might help.

Much of my early work dealt with ambiguity, and with the fact that the presence of ambiguity allows visual representations of nature to create a broader range of responses in a viewer than a careful and obvious articulation of details might. In painting this ambiguity can be achieved through painterly abstraction, the elimination of some details and the isolation of others, the removal of objects and shapes from their contexts. In photography the same kind of abstraction is achieved through cropping, the selection of parts of wholes, the use of unusual vantage points and similar devices. The *problem* of photographing with a high degree of ambiguity was based on the realization that all perception is a kind of abstraction. The attempt was to push this very real phenomenon to its limits to see what would happen. This work led to the discovery that isolated details,

objects removed from context, would often be interpreted by viewers of the representation in the same way; frequently this shared perception had nothing to do with the object that had been photographed. This *problem* of ambiguity flowed quite naturally into another, where I chose to isolate and photograph certain details which I hoped would generate specific responses – responses which, once again, really had nothing to do with the objects photographed. I photographed beams of light on dark walls, hoping to create an impression of otherworldliness. I photographed rocks which were selected because they seemed to represent visually our cultural notions of masculinity and femininity. I sought out juxtapositions of shape and tonality which could be seen as metaphorical representations of human sexuality. I exploited abstraction, but tried to use it to direct a specific response. In the process I learned a great deal about myself, and about those who viewed my work. I also learned a great deal about seeing.

This work, influenced as it was by the images of other photographers and a long-standing European tradition which intellectualized the act of making images of nature, concentrated its efforts on the relationship between ideas and those images. Continued work in nature, exposure to the fact of natural reality and my place in it, led me to the examination of a much more interesting *problem*: the attempt to represent nature apart from the imposition of ideas. This kind of seeing, more like meditation, was an attempt to deal with the similarity which exists between a photographer as natural object, and natural objects other than the photographer, and not the differences (mostly per-

ON SEEING NATURE

ceived as the difference between conscious intent and mere existing). I chose the most basic situations, and the least complex environments I could find. My *problems* became incredibly simple. Sometimes they were reduced to single words: rocks, shadows. Once again the process was important, probably more important than the products. By choosing such simple elements for attention a great deal of complexity was discarded, and the resulting images, selected for their minimal complexity, shared an astounding attribute: they were often perceived as metaphorical. The intention had been to simplify, but the images were seen as complex. Once again, I had learned something about perception and seeing. No matter how abstracted vision becomes, it exists within the context of our humanness, and of our relationship with the natural world.

The meaning of the images, of the results of the process (which has been greatly abbreviated in its description here), is not so terribly important. What is useful, and worth relating, is the pleasure of the process, and its ability to clarify vision. For the scientist the selection of problems results from training; there are few scientists who do not know the value of approaching seeing in this way. For the visual artist it seems to happen naturally, as the great complexity of the visual world finds itself abstracted in the limited representations we call art. For others the process of working with selected problems occurs, largely without conscious intent or interference, as temperament and place dictate specific concerns. For all of us the conscious exploitation of this method brings results in keener perception, and clear-

er seeing. The next time an event or object catches your interest, try to isolate your attention on similar objects and events for a while. Formulate narrow problems for yourself, and explore them. I have no doubt that the process will be enjoyable, and that if you pursue your chosen problems you will find that they grow and change as the depth of your perception grows.

In the seeing of the microcosm and the macrocosm we have an expanding and contracting perception of nature. We have the near and the far. The large and the small. The understandable and the unfathomable. Our seeing of nature moves inward, and outward, from the simple to the complex, and back again. In the process of selecting specific problems we have the same thing, but often within a more limited realm. In aesthetic vision we often have problems which have been consciously selected rather than externally imposed. In nature and the seeing of nature we have an interactive process. This process is exploited by artists, and comprises a great deal of what we have come to call aesthetic vision. We all see in this way, and we all possess the capability for aesthetic vision. We do not become artists when we learn to make pleasing representations of nature. I am not so sure that we need to have a category of people we refer to as artists at all. What matters is the ability to *see* nature. Learning to find pleasure in the *process* of seeing is part of developing that ability.

Consciously selecting specific problems, and finding pleasure in the process of learning to see, constitute a large part of aesthetic vision and help to keep both seeing and wonder alive. When Nature and the seeing of her are courted in this way, there seems to be little danger of stagnating in conservative vision. Conservative vision has as its basis the terribly incorrect notion that with sufficient experience we can know what is and what will be without ever having to look for them. I'm not sure what the connection between aesthetic vision and the analogy of the pond might be. There have been times when I have thought that the artist practices the rather radical behavior of intentionally jettisoning his existing experiential sea, and going off to search for a new one in which to place his experiences. Other times I have thought that aesthetic vision magnifies the drops of experience, purifies their essence to such an extent that no matter how large our visual and experiential seas had grown, these purified and magnified drops would change them. Maybe aesthetic vision satisfies both desires. Perhaps we have moved beyond the point where the analogy remains useful. Whatever the case, I find that the selection of specific problems and a love of process characterize aesthetic vision as much as the habit of metaphor, and that they are a great cure for the disease of conservative vision.

It seems that any conclusion we draw regarding the process of seeing immediately brings to mind an opposite conclusion with equivalent value. This is true with regard to conscious intent. As important as the selection of specific problems, and the isolation of details for attention, is the relaxing of conscious effort, and the acceptance of accidents and experiences which were neither expected nor sought. This unconscious and unintentional vision also constitutes much of what we call aesthetic vision, and it is also a significant part of everyday visual experience.

About 10 years ago I was doing a great deal of work in the desert canyon country of southeastern Utah. Anyone who has been there knows what a visual delight the area is. Its incredible sandstone formations, deep river canyons; its very special flora and fauna; the immediately recognizable microclimates, where water seeps and ferns grow, where water flows and cottonwoods bloom; the deep blue, huge and overwhelming sky; the shock of unexpectedly brilliant color (red sandstone, green juniper, fiery sunsets); these and a million other things constitute a world vastly different from the ones where most of us live. Its sparseness creates the impression of a landscape which exists to embody the notion that abstraction heightens awareness. It is a place I have loved deeply since I first saw it, and one which I have found very rewarding to photograph.

Because my photographic trips to the desert and canyonlands of Utah became regular expeditions, and because of the volume of work these trips were producing, it seemed that the most orderly and productive way to photograph would be to select individual details for attention, and to systematically move through the process of exploring the area visually. As a result, I worked on problems much in the way described above. I started with the isolation of specific objects, then specific phenomena; finally I explored metaphorical attributes. I went from sandstone formations, to plants in microclimates, to shadows, to metaphor, working always with conscious intent, hopefully in response to the landscape, but often, I fear, imposing my working framework on the existing environment. To say that this was not productive would be untrue. I learned a great deal

in the process, and generated a great many images. What was missing in this work, however, was much that constituted the unique character of the place, much that had failed to become a part of my conscious intentions. The place, fortunately, was too powerful to allow such an error to continue.

On one photographic trip to Utah, I drove my old GMC pickup with its rather Spartan camper shell to a favorite spot: an old juniper at the end of a dirt road, the beginning of a trailhead, in the Great Salt Valley of Arches National Monument. The trail that started at the juniper went over sandstone, through narrow canyons, up and down through some fairly intricate but well-travelled country. Where the trail passed over rock there were cairns at regular intervals. Where it passed over sand, the trail was quite visible. While the area was certainly not the most heavily visited in the park, it could by no means be considered wilderness. The telltale tread of running shoes (a favorite modern form of desert footware) could be found with little effort. I had chosen the trail not for its remoteness, but for the rock formations I knew to lie along its path. I had come to photograph them, to explore a visual theme which I had been pursuing for several years: the existence of metaphorical representations of masculinity and femininity in stone. It was an intriguing problem, and one which I had mined successfully for a long time.

My hike began late in the morning. Earlier that day my drive from home had taken me through the June of high altitude, the snow squalls and cold spring rains of home, to the late spring of lower elevations, and finally to the glar-

ing light and blazing hot sun of summer in the desert. As I loaded my pack for the hike, most of its space was filled with cameras, rolls of film and film holders, filters, a light meter, a cable release – the various paraphernalia of the photographer. Little space was reserved for water. I took one quart.

My hike began, and so did the photography. A few miles down the trail, several hours later, my water gone, I realized that my body was not ready for the desert. A winter in the snow had left me ill-prepared for heat. I continued to hike away from the pickup and the shade of the juniper, extending the distance between my dehydrated body and the five-gallon water bottle which sat in the camper shell. The well-marked trail became more difficult to find. It took me forever to make simple exposure calculations. I began to lose track of what I was doing, and my carefully selected visual *problems* evaporated in the brilliant sunlight. I began to see some terribly strange things in the stone, and I photographed them.

One sight in particular captivated me. In a narrow canyon, one of the few spots sheltered from the sun, a series of holes in the rock seemed to have nostrils pressed up against them from the inside. Creatures appeared to be gasping for breath, struggling to find cool air, through the holes. I photographed the rock, then paused to think. Creatures do not struggle for breath and press their nostrils against sandstone from the inside! My dehydration was much more serious than I had realized. I was hallucinating!

I sat in the shaded canyon for a while, cooled down a bit, and decided that it would be wise to terminate the photography, and make my way back to the truck, get some water in me, perhaps on me, and live to work another day. The trip back was difficult, embarrassingly so for a trail which should have been so obvious, one I had hiked several times before. Often I wandered away from the proper route and experienced great difficulty finding the trail again. When I finally made it over the bluffs which rose directly above the juniper, spotted the truck, and began the last leg of my hike to shade and water, I was filled with both relief and disgust. How could I have been so stupid!

At the time of this episode I was working for a small publishing firm, and there was precious little spare time to photograph seriously. Money for film and travel were limited. I had wasted time and money by failing to realize how abrupt the change from home to the desert would be, by failing to carry adequate water, and by continuing to expose film when my brain had apparently ceased to function.

My carefully conceived and programmed plan of visual exploration had been terminated by circumstance and stupidity. The trip appeared to have been a waste. A waste, I thought, until I saw the negatives. There, formed in an emulsion of silver and gelatin, carefully suspended over a plastic support, were the images of the desert I had made while gradually losing conscious control over the camera. Somehow the choice of exposure (and subsequent development, which had been marked on the undeveloped rolls and sheets of film) had been correct. The technical aspects of the work had gone into a kind of automatic mode. The images themselves were incredible. Surprisingly, the hallucination which had shocked me into the realization that my body was in trouble was recorded on the negatives as well. It took a little imagination to see it, but the desperate nostrils, pressed against the stone gasping for air were not entirely imagined; evidence had been recorded on film.

The time had not been wasted. Surprisingly, it had been one of the most productive photographic trips I had ever made. The negatives exposed, the things seen, had deviated from my carefully planned exploration, but an element which had long been missing had come to the work. No longer was conscious intent overpowering the existing landscape. The landscape itself had asserted its visual identity. It continued to do so later as well, even when my mental state was not one of heat- and dehydration-induced delirium. A form of control, which had initially proven useful but had become a limitation, had been left behind in the process of working, and a new vision had emerged.

In looking for ways to see, for ways to expand and clarify vision, we often seek simple formulas and techniques. Often these formulas and techniques bear fruit, but they can limit vision as well. It is true that isolating specific problems for attention can sharpen vision. It is true that a conscious program of exploration can result in a process of movement and change in our perception. When the exploration becomes too rigidly formulated, however, it becomes limiting. The relaxation of intent, and the loosening of the rules of exploration are important as well.

It is characteristic of the aesthetic process, and of aesthetic vision, that specific conscious intent is tempered with an acceptance of surprise and the unexpected. A desire for the resolution of ambiguity is mixed wonderfully with a love of the ambiguity which keeps reappearing. I believe this ongoing exploration, this love of process over resolution, wonder over certainty, characterize childlike vision as well. Perhaps an appeal to aesthetics is nothing more than an excuse to be childlike again as adults. Picasso once said that it was nothing to learn to paint an acceptable representation of something, but that to paint and see as a child once one had become an adult was a major and difficult accomplishment. To keep both wonder and vision alive we must learn, once again, to be children. We must learn not to allow our vast sea of experience to swallow up the uniqueness of each event. We must find a way to keep our experiences powerful, their color and flavor pure and undiluted. We must remain childlike.

The lesson of aesthetic vision is that of process. An acceptance of process results in a love of exploration. A love of exploration frees us from the arrogance of certainty. Any technique for seeing immediately suggests an opposite. Any conclusion, an alternative. Any resolution, a new difficulty. The critical thing is to keep moving, and to enjoy the process. Surely there are destinations and arrivals in the journey of vision. There are things to be learned and savored as accomplishments. But as any child knows, there's an awful lot to learn, and it's always too soon to stop exploring.

VI. Seeing with More Than Eyes

ABOUT A MILE from my home there is a beaver pond which sits alongside a fairly large mountain stream. Actually there are a series of such ponds, but this one in particular interests me because, for some reason unknown to me, it is the place where the largest and wariest trout of the drainage congregate during the high water of spring runoff. The insect life in this pond is amazing. Trout taken there have had stomachs filled with everything from caddis pupae to beetles. I have found fish who had eaten nothing but midge larva, and some who seem to have eaten anything which came along, including flies, bees, wasps, ants, mosquitoes and butterflies. The pond, it appears, is the trout equivalent of an all-you-can-eat smorgasbord, with the added luxury of ideal trout ambience. The water which flows through the pond is free of the silt that exists during runoff in the main stream, and also much warmer than that in the snow-melt swollen creek which roars by the calm pond. The edges of the pond are made up of an incredibly intricate maze of overhanging banks, convoluted inlets, and overgrown channels. The cover which provides protection from fish predators is abundant. In this pond the trout grow fat and, I suspect, happy. When the high water subsides, the fish leave the pond and enter the stream, but during the turbulent water of spring they collect there like collegians on break in Fort Lauderdale.

You would think, given the abundance of trout and the small size of the pond, that catching a trout in this place would be easy, but this is not the case. Several factors conspire to make the fishing difficult. The trout are wild, and extremely wary. The ground surrounding the pond consists, in most places, of a mat of vegetation which floats on underground water. Walking there disturbs the ground, and the fish. The water is crystal clear, and any fishing line on the water casts a shadow which announces, as if with neon lights and loudspeakers, the presence of a fisherman. The pond is also a haven for migrating waterfowl, mostly ducks, and any approach by a human causes a flurry of wings and frantic splashing takeoffs which alert every living thing in the area to his presence. Finally, the incredible abundance of food makes the fish less than eager to sample anything very different from what they are used to eating. This includes strangely constructed insects with hooks protruding from their abdomens.

I have fished there many times, and often been unsuccessful. When I have been successful there has usually been some help from nature, in the form of a diversion, which has allowed me to sneak up on the fish without being detected. When there has been strong wind or heavy rain to disturb the water's surface, I have been able to catch fish. Rarely, however, have I caught fish when the sky was clear, the air still, and the surface of the water calm. Occasionally I have managed to catch trout under these difficult conditions, and I think my success at those times was due to a kind of seeing which has not yet been discussed.

Whenever we analyze something we take it apart, trying to find out just exactly how it works. This works fairly well with machines. You can look at collections of gears and motors, bushings and bearings, and get a fairly good idea of what happens when the machine is assembled and working. Unfortunately, living things are not so easily understood. Having taken a living thing apart, we have not necessarily understood it. Rather, in the act of analysis we often destroy the thing we had been trying to understand. This is as true of the things creatures do, as it is of the creatures themselves. We can never understand seeing, for example, if we continue to isolate the parts of seeing. Seeing is an act committed by a living thing, a being who exists within a living world. If we are to understand seeing, we must see it whole.

One evening I arrived at the beaver pond, having frightened away a pair of nesting mallards, and every other bird in sight, to find the air still, the water calm, and the fish hiding. The sun was low in the sky but had not yet set behind the mountain to the west of the pond. Little life was apparent. Instead of flailing the water with my line and driving the fish deeper into their cover, I sat down with my back against a soft grassy hummock, and watched the scene. The first creatures to reappear were insects. I suspect they had never left, but having found me, they seemed to congregate. Midges swarmed around my head, mosquitoes dipped and landed, ants began to crawl all over me. Dressed as I was in hip waders, wind shell and cap, they really didn't bother me, so I continued to sit still. After a while the ducks returned. A pair of sandpipers strutted along the edge of the pond poking about in the muck for dinner. A red-tailed hawk appeared soaring over the pond.

More time passed, and I realized that I was enjoying this evening very much, so I continued to sit. The beaver came out for an inspection of the pond. The area was teeming with life. As the sun reached the mountain top and sank behind it, tree swallows appeared and began an aerial display. The air grew cool, the light dimmer. The swallows dipped into the water to pick emerging insects from the surface, and trout, unaware of the presence of any predator, began to pick these same insects from the water's surface from below. Several hours had passed since my arrival, since my decision to wait before casting a line. Now, I knew, was the time.

Without rising, I quietly played line from my reel into the air, and then gently dropped a small fly onto the water. Within a second of its landing, a fat trout confidently sucked it in, and, raising the tip of my rod, I found that I was fast to the fish. With steady pressure against the fish I led him into shallow water, where I freed the hook. A second cast resulted in an instant replay, with the difference that the second fish was even larger, and his struggle much more powerful. He easily pulled line off of my reel, and in a violent shake of his head, freed himself of the hook. When I recovered the fly, I saw that the hook had been straightened by the trout's actions, and by my too heavy pressure against his fight. By now the quiet had been disturbed, and no more fish appeared to be feeding. I sat for a few more minutes enjoying the evening, and finally rose to begin the walk home, knowing that I had to cross the turbulent stream which lay between the pond and my destination, and also knowing that if I waited until after dark to attempt the crossing, the trip might be a cold, wet and dangerous one.

There have been days in other places, and even at this particular pond, when I have caught substantially more fish, even larger and stronger ones, but few days spent fishing have felt as good as this one. The quality of the fishing has little to do with how large or how many. The quality of the fishing is, for me, more significantly affected by the depth of seeing and understanding achieved, and that day I saw more and understood more than usual.

Parts of that seeing make immediate sense and can be articulated. I knew, for example, that sitting still for a while would probably make the fish forget about me. I knew when the waterfowl resumed their normal behavior that at least some in the area had accepted my presence. I knew that the behavior of the swallows over the water indicated that food was available for them as well as for the trout, and that the trout would likely soon be feeding. I knew that the feeding of the trout with relative confidence would improve my chances of catching one. I knew that having an imitation of an emerging midge on my leader would make the fish think that my offering was edible. I knew these and a thousand other things. I didn't analyze them, however. My distinct memory of the event is not one of words and knowledge. It is one of sights, sounds and feelings. The swooping of the swallows, the suddenly dimmed light, the cool air, the sound of rising fish, none of these existed by itself. None of it was understood verbally. Each was a part of a moment which was one thing. A whole. I cast my fly as a part of that moment, and hooked the trout without thought. I had *seen* the moment not by wanting to analyze it, but by becoming a part of it.

We can learn a great deal about seeing by thinking about seeing. We can improve the quality of our perception by understanding and isolating the parts of the process. We must be careful not to make more of any of these parts than is appropriate, however. Oddly enough, this goes for organs and physiology as well as words and ideas. We do not see with our eyes. We do not see with our brains. We see with our entire bodies. We do not see apart from sniffing the air. We cannot see apart from feeling the ground. We do not see without compassion, or fear, or love or wonder. What is the organ of wonder? Of love? Would we dare to dissect them? At the risk of sounding absurd, I would argue even further that when we see, we see with all of nature. Without a world to see, what good are eyes? Without the relationships between organisms and objects, what is there to see? Is there any part of nature which is not somehow influenced by every other part?

There are stories told about hunters, armed with high-powered rifles and binoculars, who go off into the bush with native guides in search of game. The hunters scan the scene with their optically expanded vision looking for animals. The guides find game with their naked eyes, often at incredible distances. Even more strangely, the guides often point to animals which the hunters fail to see, even with their binoculars, until they have been flushed from their hiding places. These tales tell a great deal about the importance of seeing nature whole. The difference, you see, between the hunters and the guides is that the hunters were looking for game, individual animals, while the guides

ON SEEING NATURE

were looking for anomalies in the patterns of nature. When asked about their gift for spotting game the guides say little about visual acuity, or knowing where to look. They say things like, "The vegetation where the animal hid was dark, darker than that surrounding it; it didn't rustle." Or simply, "I knew it was there". The place was perceived in its entirety. Its sound, its smell, its sight, its very *feel*. The animal was not spotted, it wasn't isolated from its background. It was seen because of its imprint on the pattern of the whole. This kind of seeing, sounding to our educated ears a bit like mysticism, and suspect on that account, is something we all do. It is not mysticism, and it is something we all need to do more often.

I knew in the moment I cast my fly that a fish who was unaware of my presence would rise and take it. Don't ask me to explain how I knew that. I couldn't. It has more to do with the way the cool air felt on my skin, on the way the swooping swallows made me feel, than anything I had learned about trout biology.

Once we have analyzed vision, dissected its parts, worked to understand perception through careful attention to individual details, we must reassemble the parts to prevent this vivisection from killing sight altogether.

In order to see nature we must hear her, smell her, taste her and feel her. We must begin to realize that the nature we wish to know, to see, is as much a part of us as we of it. We must see nature, and ourselves, whole. We must see with more than eyes.

The idea that nature exists as a unified reality, that the fundamental *nature* of nature is singular and not fragmented, is basic to many of the world's religions. Even those which argue that there is a separation between spiritual and material reality strive to find some overriding power or being to unify the duality of matter and spirit. The seeing of this unity occurs in moments of undeniable power, often when we least expect it. It is the experience of this unified natural reality which puts our fragments together, makes our explorations meaningful, and, ultimately, brings coherence to vision.

Discussions of unified vision, of coherent perceptions of reality, often lead directly to theological discussions. I am not sure that traditional theological systems are required to unify a world which introspection has taken apart. It has been my experience that experience itself suffices.

The stream, the dappled woods, the brook trout, the child who made me see once again the importance of wonder, these were elements of a story which began this exploration of the seeing of nature. It would be fitting to conclude with them as well.

The morning of a very special day, a few years back, was spent hiking with Daniel. I don't know if it is my uncontrollable pedagogical urge, or Daniel's wonderful receptiveness to information which goads me on, but our simple hike that morning became a discourse on, and discussion of, the wonderful and complex plant we call lichen. Daniel looked at the boulders through and over which we climbed on our hike, fascinated with the brilliant orange, rich black and subtle gray-green patterns which appeared on the rocks, and asked me what they were. I told him about the lichen. I gave him a name for what he had been seeing. I told him that it was a living plant, not a single plant, really, but a complex community of two very different kinds of plants: algae and fungus. I told him about commensalism, about symbiosis; I digressed into parasitism, proceeded to elaborate on the function lichen serves in plant progression at high altitude. I told him how lichen put fibers into the surface of the rock, how they extract nourishment by dissolving the rock, and in the process break the rock down so that it can become soil. I went on to explain how lichen, simple lichen, started the complex process of creating the tundra, making a place for more varied plants to grow where there had been only rocks before. We looked up at the tundra, at the deep green carpet of ground-hugging plants which hung onto the mountain, maintaining life in the difficult conditions of high altitude. I spoke, he listened. Occasionally he asked questions. With each answer his eyes grew wider, as the intricate tapestry which contains all living things became more and more visible to him. Finally we stopped talking, smiled at each other, and walked on in silence. Lost in our own thoughts, but enjoying each other's company, we hiked. After a while it dawned on me that Daniel was lagging behind a bit farther than usual. He seemed to be pausing at every large rock, every evidence of lichen. He was touching the rocks and saying something. I stopped to wait for him, and as he came near, I saw him pause, lovingly pat a rock, and say, "I like lichen." Then he looked up at me and smiled.

We returned home. I went to work. Later that evening I went off by myself to fish for a few hours in Lime Creek. The woods were lovely as usual, and the sound and feel of the rushing water a wonderful antidote to the pressures of the day. The stretch of water I fished was chosen more for the beauty of the spot than for the fishing. It was a place I often came to in order to refresh my spirit and find peace. In this place the creek flows through aspen as a wide, smooth glide. Sunlight filters through the trees and splashes on the forest floor, broken and brilliant. The white trunks of the trees glow as if illuminated from the inside. The fallen leaves of seasons past litter the forest and crunch as you walk. Few places are as beautiful, or as soothing.

I fished through the broad glide of water, catching a few trout, and worked my way upstream past the glide, through a rapid, into a pool. After working the pool, and catching a few more trout, I realized that the sun had set, and the woods were growing dark. Twilight Peak, which towered above me, was bathed in the red light called alpenglow. Reluctantly I left the water, and started the walk through the woods back to my car. When I reached the glide, before turning away from the stream, I knelt down for a drink of water. When I looked up from the stream, I saw a solitary mule deer across the water who had come to drink and had looked up at the same moment as I. We stared into each other's eyes for what seemed an eternity. As we stared, distinctions became blurred. We shared the woods. We shared the water. We shared the surprise of seeing another when we thought we had been alone. For a moment it was difficult to remember that I was the human and he was the wild creature. The differences between us did not seem so terribly great.

The spot where this occurred was within a few feet of the place where Daniel had held and released so many brook trout, where years ago I had looked into his eyes and seen his wonder. Now I was looking into the eyes of a deer, and he was looking into mine. I remembered Daniel's loving pats on the rocks that morning, and his touching words, "I like lichen." I thought about our natural predilection for wonder, our connection with our genetic past, our inborn love of living things and of the natural world. I thought about the creation and evolution of the world, about the development of habitats and of communities of beings, about communication between people and between species, about empathy and the arrogance of anthropomorphism. I thought about sublimity and beauty. I thought about these and a million other things I have forgotten. I thought about them in an instant. I didn't so much think them as know them. I saw that deer, and myself, and this place in the woods. I saw that moment in time as an element, and a whole. I saw it for what it was: a momentary reflection of the timeless unity which is nature.

Slowly I rose, and, glancing back across the stream, walked to my car, to the road, to less immediate perceptions and less powerful visions. But I was not saddened by the loss of intensity. One cannot live at that level of perception constantly. I knew that there would be more such moments in my life, more wonderful moments when I would not simply look, but see.

LIST OF PHOTOGRAPHS